**Theatre
Centre**

The Muddy Choir

Jesse Briton

First performed at Redbridge Drama Centre
11 September 2014

The Muddy Choir

Cast

Will: **Lawrence Russell**
Robbie: **Ryan Penny**
Jumbo: **Andrew Burrell**

Creative Team

Director: **Natalie Wilson**
Dramaturg: **Douglas Maxwell**
Designer: **Emma Donovan**
Lighting Designer: **Charlie Lucas**
Sound Designer: **Elena Peña**
Musical Director / Arranger: **Zara Nunn**
Composer: **Max Mackintosh**
Voice Coach: **Jonathan Dawes**
Production Manager: **Mark Lovell**
Company Stage Manager: **Joseph Colgan**

Theatre Centre Staff

Artistic Director: **Natalie Wilson**
General Manager: **Charles Bishop**
Schools Producer: **Marigold Hughes**
Office and Tour Coordinator: **Sarah Setter**
Marketing Manager: **Tom Davies**

Theatre Centre, Shoreditch Town Hall,
380 Old Street, London EC1V 9LT
Telephone: 020 7729 3066
www.theatre-centre.co.uk

Company No: 0585723 (England & Wales) | Charity No: 210262

Writer's Note
Jesse Briton

It's important that this play is not viewed as historical fact. To the best of my knowledge the events depicted within have no relation in real life. For a playwright working today to try and capture the reality of trench warfare is, at least in my opinion, impossible. I was not there to experience it and chances are neither were you. I have tried with research, knowledge of their background, good guidance and my own imagination to bring these three boys to life. If we are successful we might also have captured something of the spirit of that time and place.

Raking over the already well-worn ground of the First World War, it's difficult to see what else can be added. Much more so when research throws up the inconvenient 'theatrical' truth that much of trench life was actually rather tedious and boring. But while I cannot know the reality of that war, I live in a world still troubled by conflict. From which I can gather only that innocence is lost, on all sides. It was not clear to me until the very end what I was writing. A play about choice, I think, as I guess they all are.

Director's Introduction
Natalie Wilson

Commissioning a new play is a high-risk game. It's partly a highly controlled and considered decision and partly a wild leap of faith. Any commissioning decision Theatre Centre makes is a long-term commitment; I have to work with the writer, the story and the writing process for nearly two years before it comes to the stage.

Yet it never fails to amaze me that I never know when the process will start. *The Muddy Choir* started one summer afternoon. I had gone to see a production of *There Is Only One Wayne Matthews* by Roy Williams at Southwark Playhouse. Scanning the promo leaflets, my eyes landed on a striking image of a young man in a sou'wester being drenched by water in a dynamic visual shot. The copy was intriguing, a new play by a company that focused on narrative and song. I was curious enough to buy a ticket. Fast forward a few weeks and I came out of the play *Bound* by Jesse Briton completely buzzing. It was a taut, compelling story of desperate fishermen caught in a storm of life and death. The stirring sea shanties sung by the cast heightened the drama and I was hooked.

I had been considering a commission to commemorate the First World War and finding Jesse sealed the deal. The right writer had stepped into my world. I knew that there would be a lot of material around the War, but I was keen to have a new play written that embraced the stories of the teenage young men in the trenches, moving us on from the more common discourses of the war poets, *War Horse* and *Blackadder*. I wanted us to see the 'Great War' from perspective of young characters that the young people in school could recognise as themselves; that they could relate to and connect with. I wasn't too concerned with the history lesson that a play might offer; many other art works and programmes have provided that. I wanted to present the teenage face of the whole catastrophe that was 1914–18, possibly by reluctant participants, drawn into it because that was what was expected of young men at the time. I knew Jesse could write these young men incredibly well with utter truth and confidence. I gave him the licence to invent a new story that could reflect a young person's sense of the pressure, the fear, and the sacrifice.

Theatre Centre in its recent plays has travelled the contemporary world, from the streets of the London riots to the rainforests of Brazil to the devastation of Hurricane Katrina. However, this play looks back in time to a different age, one of comradeship, trench culture, gas and mud. But by taking a fresh look at the era of the First World War through this classical new play, we hope to allow audiences to see themselves or their friends reflected in the characters and ask the question: How would I have survived? What choices would I make to ensure that my friends and I came through? What would I sacrifice in order to live and to live with myself?

Jesse Briton, Playwright

Jesse is the founder and Artistic Director of Bear Trap Theatre Company. His first play, *Bound*, won a Fringe First in 2010 and a nomination for the *Evening Standard* Award for Most Promising Playwright in 2011. Bear Trap recently premiered *Enduring Song* at the Southwark Playhouse, and Jesse is currently developing a new play *A Pupil* for the company. His work as an actor includes the world tour of *Potted Potter*, and *Humans* for Schouwburg Theatre, Rotterdam and BAM, New York. He is a visiting director at East 15.

Natalie Wilson, Director

Natalie studied Theatre Studies at Glasgow University. She was awarded a Scottish Arts Council Trainee Director Bursary with 7:84 (Scotland) before becoming Associate Director at the New Vic Theatre, Newcastle-under-Lyme. As a freelance director, Natalie has worked with many companies and drama schools as well as festivals and events including *Glasgay!*, *queerupnorth*, and *Manchester Pride*. She set up Truant Company in 2005, and was appointed Artistic Director of Theatre Centre in 2007, leading the company into its sixtieth year and beyond.

Her directing credits include: *Valley Song* (7:84), *Travels With My Aunt*, *Loot*, *East is East* (New Vic), *Amy's View* (Salisbury Playhouse), *Beautiful Thing* (Nottingham Playhouse), *Brighton Beach Memoirs* (Oldham Coliseum), *Smilin' Through*, *Forward* (Birmingham Rep/ Contact Theatre), *Martha Loves Michael* (Pleasance, Edinburgh Fringe), *Rigged*, *The Day the Waters Came*, *Advice for the Young at Heart* (Theatre Centre). In 2011, she was awarded a New Writing Encouragement Award by the Writers Guild of Great Britain.

Lawrence Russell (Will)

Lawrence trained at East 15 Acting School under Andrea Brooks. Since graduating, he has worked in film, voice over and theatre, and was awarded NSDF Commendations for Acting and Writing at the Edinburgh Fringe. Lawrence also regularly writes and performs for the *Happy Idiot* YouTube sketch channel.

Theatre includes: Manuel in *Fawlty Towers Dinner Show* (tour); Gerald, *When We Are Married*; Tom in *Breakfast at Dalkey* (Brighton Fringe); John in *The Lift* (Edinburgh Fringe); James in *Rathmore's Whippet* (Edinburgh Fringe); Laertes in *Hamlet* (East 15), Trofimov in *The Cherry Orchard* (East 15).

Ryan Penny (Robbie)

Training: Mountview Academy of Theatre Arts. Theatre includes: Richard in *Detrimental* (Vertical Line); David in *Sandel* (Edinburgh). Short film includes: Ed in *Waterbird* (Nightingale Productions). Theatre while training includes: Ben in *Days of Significance*; William in *Cressida*; Calpurnia/Lucius/Publius in *Julius Caesar.*

Andrew Burrell (Jumbo)

Andrew trained at Guildford School of Acting. His credits include the workshop of the new musical *Super Ordinary* (Soho Theatre), *Joseph and the Amazing Technicolor Dreamcoat* (UK tour) and *Elegies for Angels, Punks and Raging Queens* (Theatro Technis, Camden).

Creative team

Douglas Maxwell, Dramaturg

Douglas Maxwell's plays have been performed in translation in
Germany, Norway, Hong Kong, New York, France, Chicago,
Holland, Sweden, New Zealand, Wales, Canada, Japan and South
Korea, where his debut play *Our Bad Magnet* has been running
for over ten years. His plays for young people include *Helmet*,
Mancub, *Too Fast* and *Miracle Man*. *The Mother Ship* won the
Brian Way Award for Best Play for Young People in 2009, presented
by Theatre Centre. His iconic, multi-award winning play *Decky
Does a Bronco* has been revived many times since its debut in
2000. The *Scotsman* called it 'one of the finest plays to emerge
from a Scottish working-class story in the last ten years'. He has
been dramaturg on many projects for companies such as the
National Theatre of Scotland, Random Accomplice, David Leddy
and Summerhall.

Emma Donovan, Designer

Has designed over 150 productions. Some credits include: *Kes*
(Cast Doncaster); *Sing Yer Heart Out for the Lads*, *Abigail's Party*,
The *Importance of Being Earnest* (Pilot Theatre /York Theatre
Royal); *Eugène Onegin* (Scottish Opera); *Smilin' Through*,
Forward (Birmingham Rep Theatre). Emma also works as a
designer and consultant on archicitectural restorations.

Charlie Lucas, Lighting Designer

Charlie trained at RADA. His lighting designs include *Advice for
the Young at Heart* (Theatre Centre), *The Match Box* (Liverpool
Playhouse and Tricycle), *Equally Divided*, *Mother Goose* (Watford
Palace), *The Magic Flute* (Garsington Opera), *Von Ribbentrop's
Watch* (Oxford Playhouse), *Cautionary Tales* (Opera North),
Jealousy (The Print Room), *Red Riding Hood* (Theatre Royal
Stratford East).

Elena Peña, Sound Designer/Composer

Elena is an Associate Artist for Inspector Sands, with whom she has designed *A High Street Odyssey*, *Mass Observation*, *Rock Pool*, *A Life in 22 Minutes*, *A Portrait of the Ordinary Festival-Goer* and *If That's All There Is*. Other sound design credits include: *Flashes* (Young Vic), *Brimstone and Treacle* (Arcola Theatre), *Twelve Years* (BBC Radio 4 Drama), *Gambling* (Soho Theatre), *The 13 Midnight Challenges of Angelus Diablo* (RSC), *Quimeras* (Sadlers Wells, Edinburgh International Festival), *Unbroken* (Gate Theatre) and *Plasticine* (Southwark Playhouse).

Zara Nunn, Musical Director / Arranger

Zara trained at the University of Glamorgan, Royal Welsh College of Music and Drama and London College of Music. When not musically directing or composing for professional theatre, Zara works extensively in music and theatre education and specialises in major large-scale devising and performance projects. She is currently on staff as a member of the singing faculty at the award-winning MTA and she also specialises in bespoke devised music theatre projects for young people.

Credits (musical director, composer, various) include: *The Tempest* (Watford Palace); *Alice in Wonderland*, *The Lion, the Witch and the Wardrobe* (Royal & Derngate); *Aladdin*, *Dick Whittington*, *Cinderella*, *Telling Tales*, *Jack and the Beanstalk*, *The Scarlet Pimpernel*, *Much Ado About Nothing*, *Sleeping Beauty* (Everyman Theatre, Cheltenham); *The Good Egg*; *Oh! What a Lovely War*, *Common Chorus* (Royal Central School of Speech and Drama); *Arabian Nights*, *Peter Pan*, *Alice*, *The Doctor's Daughter*, *The Greek*, *The Life of Pi*, *The Grimms' Tales*; *An Artist and a Mariner*; *A Time Machine* (Royal Central School of Speech and Drama at the Minack).

Theatre Centre has worked tirelessly since 1953 to produce high-quality live theatre for young audiences across the UK. The company commissions established and emerging playwrights to create stories that are captivating, thrilling and provocative for children and young people at the very beginning of a relationship with the performing arts. With a particular focus on performing in school halls and other locations familiar to young people, Theatre Centre's aim is to demonstrate the inspirational nature of live

Theatre Centre

performance, and to encourage creativity in thought, learning and artistic practice.

The company also looks to the future of theatre for young people, supporting emerging writers through the Skylines section of the Theatre Centre website – containing resources, interviews and insights from playwrights and devisers experienced in creating work for under-18s – and through a series of awards and attachments.

Theatre Centre is a registered charity, and is a National Portfolio Organisation supported by Arts Council England.

'I loved the performance today at my school. It was very hard not to cry at some parts, but also hard not to laugh too loud.'
Jamie, audience member

'At the performance I was at, there were scores of kids from the inner city. They stood and cheered as the characters confronted the evils in their midst. Above all, they found it authentic.'
Alan White, *New Statesman*

'The time, effort and care they take over the writers' work is in my experience second to none.'   Jesse Briton, playwright

'Theatre Centre is providing a hugely valuable service to young people. Giving air time to important subjects, prompting deep thought and inspiring young people with high quality productions, it really benefits young people, emotionally as well as educationally.'
Polly Courtney, novelist

LOTTERY FUNDED

Supported using public funding by
ARTS COUNCIL ENGLAND

Every new piece of writing Theatre Centre commissions provides teachers with a powerful means by which they can explore pressing and immediate topics with students. Theatre Centre productions support National Curriculum requirements across a range of subjects – through live engagement and the provision of comprehensive learning resources made available online.

Theatre Centre Education

With all Theatre Centre shows, schools can book post-show workshops and Q&A sessions for students. Continuing Professional Development opportunities for teachers are also offered.

Teachers can also utilise a range of free resources and lesson plans, available from Theatre Centre's website. These are designed to help teachers get maximum value from the performance. Visit **www.theatre-centre.org.uk/education** to download and begin using these today.

Keeping in touch

News and information about Theatre Centre shows and projects is kept online at **www.theatre-centre.co.uk**, alongside a comprehensive archive with images and insight into over sixty years of shows.

Theatre Centre is also active on social media, so 'like' the company on Facebook or follow it on Twitter:
https://www.facebook.com/TheatreCentreUK
https://twitter.com/TCLive

New for this tour is an Instagram account, where audiences can join the conversation and take part:
http://instagram.com/theatrecentre/

For enquiries about bookings, or partnership opportunities, email:
admin@theatre-centre.co.uk

And finally, to keep up-to-date with all the latest, join the email list at
http://www.theatre-centre.co.uk/mailing-list/

The Muddy Choir

Jesse Briton grew up in Somerset before training on East 15 Acting School's Contemporary Theatre course under Uri Roodner. As founder and artistic director of Bear Trap Theatre Company, he has written and directed two original works: *Bound*, which won a Fringe First and a nomination for the *Evening Standard* Award for Most Promising Playwright, and *Enduring Song*, first performed at Southwark Playhouse in 2014. Commissioned work includes *Movere* for Curious Directive. His work as an actor includes the world tour of *Potted Potter* and *The Humans* for Schouwburg Theatre, Rotterdam and BAM, New York. He is a visiting director at East 15 Acting School and co-producer of Wassail.

JESSE BRITON

The Muddy Choir

FABER & FABER

First published in 2014
by Faber and Faber Limited
74–77 Great Russell Street, London WC1B 3DA

Typeset by Country Setting, Kingsdown, Kent CT14 8ES
Printed in England by CPI Group (UK) Ltd, Croydon CR0 4YY

A CIP record for this book is available from the British Library

ISBN 978-0-571-32288-6

FSC
www.fsc.org
MIX
Paper from
responsible sources
FSC® C013604

2 4 6 8 10 9 7 5 3 1

The Muddy Choir, a Theatre Centre production, began a national tour at the Redbridge Drama Centre, London, on 11 September 2014. The cast was as follows:

Will Jones Lawrence Russell
Robbie Mitchell Ryan Penny
Jumbo Wallis Andrew Burrell

Director Natalie Wilson
Dramaturg Douglas Maxwell
Designer Emma Donovan
Lighting Designer Charlie Lucas
Sound Designer Elena Peña
Musical Director / Arranger Zara Nunn
Composer Max Mackintosh
Voice Coach Jonathan Dawes
Production Manager Mark Lovell
Company Stage Manager Joseph Colgan

Characters

Will Jones
Lance Corporal

Robbie Mitchell
Private

Jumbo Wallis
Private

ONE

A trench. Lance Corporal Will Jones, Private Robbie Mitchell and Private Jumbo Wallis, three teenage conscripts and childhood friends from Sunderland, stand with their backs to us and prepare for action.

Robbie Alreet, now y' remember how we practised? We're deeing it just like that. Straight doon the line, hitting it all, nowt missed. Nee wobbles or deviations. I divn't wanta hear anyone lost or left behind. Nee matter what happens we stay together. The pace will be fast but that's how it's meant t' be. It's the three of us together just like it's always been. Ready?

Will This is a bad idea . . .

Robbie On my count.

Will Rob . . .

Robbie One, two, three, four.

Jumbo and Robbie turn and sing.

LAMBTON WORM

One Sunday morn young Lambton went
   A-fishing' in the Wear;
An' catched a fish upon he's heuk,
   He thowt leuk't varry queer.
But what'n a kind of fish it was
   Yang Lambton cudden't tell.
He waddn't fash te carry'd hyem,
   So he hoyed it doon a well.

Whisht! Lads, haad yor gobs,
    An Aa'll tell ye's aall an aaful story
Whisht! Lads, haad yor gobs,
    An' Aa'll tell ye 'boot the worm.

Will Incoming!

Explosions ring out. They dive to the floor.

Stay doon! Stay doon!

Explosions continue and then stop. Will looks up.

All clear!

They rise to their feet.

I telt y' singing were a bad idea! Only been in the new observation post five bloody minutes and already y' playing the fool! You want t' get us kicked back doon the line?

Jumbo Ee, I loved it! Just what I needed! Not done that for a while, have we? Took us right back t' before the war, right back t' Sunderland: the clanging of the shipyards, the view from the weir as a new ship floats out on to the North Sea and the smell of me mam's pies . . . Oooh, pies! There's a thought, Will! Y' fancy a pie?

Will No, Jumbo, that's alreet. I'll just be up here checking your singing didn't start another war.

He takes up a position overlooking the front.

Jumbo Rob?

Robbie Yes?

Jumbo Pie?

Robbie No.

Jumbo Oh, gan on!

Robbie Seriously, Jumbo, where y' ganne get a pie from round here, eh? Y' seen any just lying around?

Jumbo I bet Will could get one for us. Will can de anything! Got us off the line and into this cushy observation post, didn't he? Oot'a the wet and cold. Nice little digs all t' owerselves!

Robbie Easy, Jumbo. It's hardly paradise, is it? Look, the last lad left his kit strewn all awer the place.

Will I'll take that.

Will picks up remaining kit as Robbie continues his analysis.

Robbie The walls are leaky. There's ne roof.

Jumbo None of the trenches have a roof, Rob.

Robbie The officers de! And look at the floor!

Robbie lifts up his shoes to expose the sole. He points to it.

It's covered in rat sh—

Jumbo Hey, we've got extra rations too!

Jumbo holds up the rations.

Robbie Oh, another tin of ham? I could have done without another tin a' ham, Jumbo.

Will Really?

Robbie Aye.

Will Well I'll just take it back then, shall I?

Will reaches for the ham but Robbie pulls it away from him.

Robbie . . . No.

Will Ahh, I thought so.

He turns back to the front.

Jumbo Oh, and look!

He points at Will's arm.

He even got himself a promotion! Not bad for a simple lad from our neck of the woods eh, Rob? Y' must be proud?

Robbie Oh, I'm overflowing wi' pride, Jumbo. I bet he had t' de summit reet special for that.

Jumbo Aye, summit super special nee doubt! Grand job, Will!

Will Thanks, Jumbo. Nice t' have some appreciation for a change.

Jumbo (*salutes Will*) Nee bother!

He turns to Robbie.

So, what d'you make of the new post, Rob?

Robbie Looks pretty much like the last one if y' ask me, and the one before that, and the one before that too. In fact, it looks pretty much like everywhere we've been in France.

Will This isn't France any more, lads. This is Flanders.

Jumbo Hang aboot, we're not in France?

Will No, welcome to Passchendaele.

He gestures to the front.

Just a stone's throw from Wipers.

Jumbo When did we leave France?

Will We crossed the border last week.

Jumbo I divn't remember that.

Will We were being bombed at the time, Jumbo. We had more important things to worry aboot.

Jumbo Oh. Well, nice to be in Belgium, I suppose. That's another one ticked off the list. Mam will be dead excited. Getting plenty a' travel in at least.

Jumbo takes a big inhale of Belgian air.

Ahhh, Belgium.

Will laughs.

Robbie Well, it all looks the bloody same with these eyes: muddy, brown and smelly.

Will That's one way t' look at it.

Robbie Oh, right. Tell us another then, Will. I'm all ears.

Will Well, we're off the main line for one. Ne more curling up next to thirty other lads in a trench. Less bombs, more rations, and we've even got a more specialised role: observing gunfire and enemy movement: a highly prestigious job.

Robbie Oh, is that what you're deeing up there? Looking for prestige?

Jumbo What does prestige mean?

Robbie It means sacrificing y' principles to advance y' social status, Jumbo.

Jumbo What does that mean?

Robbie points at Will.

Robbie Him.

Jumbo I divn't understand.

Will Say what y' like, Robbie. But I divn't see ye deing anything t'get us through this.

Robbie folds his arms.

Robbie Wasn't my choice t' be here.

Will It wasn't anyone's choice t' be here, Rob. That's what conscription means. They pick you, not the other way round. Your country calls and you have to answer.

Robbie Bloody unfair if y'ask me.

Will No one is. Now if y' divnt mind I have t'acquaint m'self with the lay o' the land. We're an observation post now.

Robbie So?

Will We have to observe.

Jumbo From the post!

Will Cheers, Jumbo.

Robbie (*mocking Will*) Cheers, Jumbo!

Jumbo Oh give over, Rob man.

Robbie Can you see owt special then?

Will Just a load a' shell craters.

Robbie Fascinating! Yet another invaluable insight from our man at the front: only the very freshest information from him! Tell us, Lance Corporal, de'ya think the war has much left in it? Can y' see an end to it through y' battlefield spectacles? Will it be awer by Christmas 1914?

Jumbo It's 1917, Rob . . .

Robbie Oh God, I kna, Jumbo! I was trying t' make a joke! You remember those? God, you'll be the death of us, literally and comedically.

Will I divn't think you'll need any help with that, Rob.

Robbie Oh, another joker! How lucky we are! Three in one trench! I'm laughing so hard it hurts! My sides are literally splitting! Ha, ha, ha!

Will Are y' finished, Rob?

Robbie Just aboot.

Will Good. Then let's get back to work, shall we? Get y' kit away and I'll draw up a rota for watch.

Robbie Great idea. You crack on with that and we'll bash out another song. Jumbo?

Jumbo Aye, count me in!

Will No! Enough singing! War isn't the place for singing, Rob. Y' kna this, I shouldn't have t' explain it.

Robbie No, Will. Man's got a right t' sing, and neebody can take that away from him. Y' used to kna that. Singing is natural. All of this, all of *this*, ain't.

Will And what if y' singing attracts the enemy's attention?

Robbie They kna we're here, Will! It's not like they'll hear us and suddenly realise the whole British army has been sleeping under their noses! (*German accent.*) Was is das? Is zer English aboot? Ven did ze arrive? We ver just trying to have zis picnic! What war? Zer is no war!

Jumbo laughs.

Jumbo Good one!

Will There's a careful balance in place. Ne side attacks unless they have te. We divn't wanna set things off.

Robbie Oh, what are they ganne de? Get scared of a couple ditties? Isn't that kind of the point of fighting anyway? To intimidate the opponent? Besides, I'm sure you can take care of us all, Will. Big strong army captain man!

Will I'm not a captain. I'm a lance corporal.

Robbie Same thing.

Jumbo Oh, wait! We should de the pledge!

Robbie *and* **Will** The pledge?

Jumbo Aye! We've not done it in ages!

Robbie That's not true. I hear y' de it every night.

Jumbo Aye, but that's just me. We've not done it as a group since . . . for ever. Haways, what d'ya think?

Beat.

Will Maybe next time.

Will turns back to the front.

Jumbo Will . . .

Robbie Oh, let him sulk, lad. I'll dee it wi' ya. Ready?

Jumbo nods. They both inhale.

Jumbo *and* **Robbie** Nee killing. Anly singing. And we all gan home together.

Jumbo hugs Robbie.

Jumbo Cheers, Rob.

Robbie Nee problem, lad. Now, y' ready?

Jumbo Aye.

Robbie One, two, three, four . . .

They hit the first note. Cue sound of incoming fire.

Will Get doon!

TWO

Jumbo and Robbie curled up on the trench floor. Robbie is using a small mirror, comb and spit to style his hair. Jumbo is trying to sleep; occasionally he scratches himself and wriggles from side to side, each time he does it disturbs Robbie.

Robbie Will y' stop bloody wriggling man!

Jumbo I cannet! It's the lice!

Robbie Burn them off then!

Jumbo I divn't kna how!

Robbie You've watched me de it millions of times!

Jumbo I forget!

Robbie Then put up and shut up!

Jumbo I'm trying!

They resume their previous positions until Jumbo begins scratching again. Robbie is frustrated again, but tries to hide it.

Rob?

Robbie Aye.

Jumbo Where's Will?

Robbie Kissing the Sergeant Major's arse probably.

Jumbo continues scratching.

Jumbo Rob?

Robbie Aye.

Jumbo You ever think aboot home?

Robbie What else is there to de?

Jumbo What d'ya think aboot when y' think a' home?

Robbie What do I think aboot?

Jumbo Aye, tell us.

Robbie thinks.

Robbie The things I miss.

Jumbo Like?

Robbie My own space!

He gives Jumbo a push.

Jumbo You miss y' bedroom? I miss my bedroom.

Robbie Jumbo, your bedroom was aboot the size a' this trench.

Jumbo Aye.

Robbie And it had all y' brothers and sisters sleeping in it.

Jumbo Just like this trench.

He smiles at Robbie.

Robbie Oh God . . .

Jumbo laughs.

Jumbo What else?

Robbie Jumbo . . .

Jumbo Come on, what else?

Robbie The girls. I miss the girls.

Jumbo Oh, aye. The girls . . .

They get lost in wistful reminiscence.

And me mam. I miss me mam too.

Robbie Aye, I miss y' mam an' all.

Jumbo Robbie!

Jumbo shoves Robbie. He just laughs.

Robbie And the clubs of course. Oh God, I miss the clubs. The music, the girls, the suits, the dresses, the girls, the lights, the girls, the dancing, the girls.

Jumbo continues scratching and Robbie loses it.

Right! That's it! Enough is enough! I won't have y' wriggling around like a fat little mouse behind me! Shirt off!

Jumbo It's not me shirt, it's me trousers . . .

Robbie looks at Jumbo.

Robbie Really?

Jumbo shrugs hopelessly.

Fine. Trousers off.

Jumbo removes his trousers and hands them to Robbie.

Candle.

Jumbo locates his candle and passes it to Robbie.

Jumbo Thanks, Rob.

Robbie Divn't mention it. I mean seriously, divn't mention it, t' anyone!

Jumbo nods. Robbie lights a match and with it the candle. He holds both up to his face and looks at Jumbo.

Let's gan hunt'n!

Jumbo cheers. Will enters. Robbie and Jumbo freeze. Will takes in the scene around him.

Will Having fun?

Jumbo raises his pants.

Jumbo Hunting for lice.

Will considers them.

Will Carry on.

Robbie salutes sarcastically.

Robbie Aye, sir.

Will stares at him, but Robbie ignores him and continues delousing.

Will I'm not an officer, Rob. Y' divn't have t' sir me.

Robbie Sorry, I get confused.

Jumbo Where've y' been, Will?

Will With the Sergeant Major.

Robbie Makes a change.

Jumbo He say anything interesting?

Will Yes, actually.

Robbie Oh. Let me guess . . . he loves you?

Will No.

Jumbo The war's over?

Will Not quite. He said our lads intercepted a communiqué from the other side. A message from one of their commanders saying he overheard singing from our trench and used it as guide for targeting.

Jumbo and Robbie look at Will.

He asked if we'd been singing.

Jumbo What did y' say?

Will I telt him I'd heard nowt.

Jumbo Did he believe you?

Will No.

Will takes a letter from his pocket and holds it out for them.

He gave us this.

They look at it.

Robbie What's that?

Will A letter.

Jumbo What's in it?

Will A name.

Jumbo Good, Will's a crap one!

Jumbo looks for the laugh. He doesn't get it. Will reads from the letter.

Will Alexander Pattison.

Jumbo What's special aboot him?

Will Alexander died fifteen minutes ago. Killed instantly when a Kraut shell hit his dugout. They were trying t' stop us singing and missed. That shell was aimed at us but hit Alexander.

A pause.

Jumbo Oh God.

A pause.

Oh God.

Robbie What was his name again?

Will Alexander Pattison.

Will hands Robbie the letter for him to examine.

Jumbo Oh God.

Robbie Where was he from?

Will Our side a' the wear. Hendon.

Jumbo Oh God.

Robbie What road?

Will Percy Terrace.

Robbie turns to Jumbo.

Robbie That's one away from you.

Jumbo Oh God . . .

Pause.

Robbie What d'we de now?

Will Sergeant Major said the death of an enlisted man resulting from friendly action means someone has t' gan before a court-martial.

Jumbo They're putting us on trial?

Will That's the plan. He said they need time t' get the appropriate people together but then one, or all of us, will have t' report for charges.

Jumbo What will they de t' us?

Will If we're found guilty they'll want t' make an example of us. Restore discipline and all that.

Jumbo What, prison?

Will Worse.

Robbie Firing squad.

Jumbo looks at Robbie, then back to Will.

Jumbo Oh God. We're done for . . .

Will Maybe not. After he gave me Alexander's name he told me the generals are planning a huge surprise advance across the line t' catch Fritz whilst he's sleeping. He said that if by some chance the Kraut guns were aimed away from the attack at another part of the line, say, a sparsely but handsomely manned observation post, it would not be 'entirely unhelpful'. De that and the court-martial papers get lost in the post. His words.

Pause.

Jumbo Wait. What are y' saying? He wants us as bait? He wants us t' get bombed deliberately?

Will That's the deal.

Jumbo How?

Will Same as last time. Singing.

Jumbo Singing?

Will Singing.

Pause.

Robbie Sod. That.

Robbie stands.

Nah, lads. I'm not having this! He's gan too far this time!
Divn't worry, I'm gonna sort this one oot face t' face!

Robbie rolls up his sleeves and steps towards the exit.

Time for a little word with our Sergeant Major . . .

Will stands in front of him.

Will . . . ?

Will They're orders.

Robbie What?

Will Orders is orders. Y' singing.

THREE

*Will is in position overlooking no-man's-land, Jumbo
sitting on the floor cleaning his rifle, Robbie shaking his
head in the corner.*

Will Look, we've been gannen awer the same point for
hours now. I've already telt ya y' singing. Now crack on
and help Jumbo wi' the cleaning.

Robbie Oh, I'll crack on, Will, divn't y' worry, but there's
still one thing I'm a bit confused aboot.

Will (*sighing*) Aye?

Robbie Y' see, I remember you saying that singing was a stupid idea. Y' did say that didn't ya? He did say that didn't he, Jumbo?

Jumbo Sorry, Will, but y' did.

Will The situation's changed.

He turns back to the front.

Robbie So singing for fun isn't allowed, but singing for war is?

Will Sergeant Major's orders, not mine.

Robbie Oh, so when the Sergeant Major says it's alreet, it's alreet. But when y' best mate says it's alreet, it's not? Oh, thanks a bunch, Will. Nice to kna where y' real loyalty lies. I see not much has changed since school, eh? Still the bloody teacher's pet!

Will We're not in school any more, Rob. We're in a war. We're in an army and we have t' follow the chain of command if we want t' survive.

Robbie Sounds like the head boy again t' me. Bloody swot.

Jumbo Give over, Robbie. Will's always looked out for us, hasn't he?

Robbie Oh, on his side again, Jumbo? I guess we are back at school!

Will turns to them.

Will Our signal will be three clear whistles. We're ordered t' start singing straight after. We cannet leave it a second later or we'll miss the window and the assault will gan in under fire. Everything has t' be synchronised perfectly. We're a vital part of the officers' plans.

Robbie Oh, good. I've always wanted t' be a vital part of the officers' plans.

Will Alexander is dead, Robbie. Divn't forget that.

He turns back to the front.

Robbie Divn't we get a say in it?

Will No.

Robbie What if I divn't de it?

Will Then we'll all get court-martialled and put in front of a firing squad. You want that for y' mates?

Robbie So either way it's suicide? We might as well throw ourselves awer the bloody top right now!

Will Aye, that'd be a shame though.

Robbie Aww, you'd miss us?

Will I wouldn't, but the officers might.

Robbie What?

Will They're dead excited t' hear you sing. Some idiot told them you've got the best voice in the whole of Ypres.

Jumbo Oh Robbie, that's great news!

Robbie Alreet, now I kna' y' lying!

Will God's honest truth. Hand on heart. Y' kna I didn't tell 'em 'cause I divn't actually think you've got the best voice in Ypres. A bit shrill, if you ask me, too nasal.

Robbie Oh, very funny!

Will Honest. I've heard lads doon the line with much better singing voices than you . . .

Robbie Not true!

Will Just saying . . .

Robbie So what? I've performed in front of officers before. I divn't care aboot them anyway. I prefer real people, Will. Singing t' real people.

Will Aye, but can real people get you on a boat back across the Channel?

Beat.

Jumbo They'll send us home?

Will If we save the advance. They're always on the lookout for a good morale story. And there's nothing like three strapping lads carrying out a daring mission to draw enemy fire, especially if they're singing. Aye, they'll probably de pictures of us. Proper paintings like. With medals . . .

Jumbo Medals?

Will Aye, nee doubt. VC stuff, this is. That's a big shiny one.

Jumbo Ee, me mam would love that!

Will Exactly, Jumbo. That's the whole point, summit t'inspire the folks back home and make the ladies blush.

Jumbo Make the ladies blush?

Will Think aboot it this way, Jumbo, how many times have y' been shot at?

Jumbo Dunno.

Will If you had t' guess?

Jumbo A lot.

Will And how many times have y' been shelled?

Jumbo A lot.

Will And gassed?

Jumbo Slightly less: but still quite a lot.

Will Right. Now, the way I see it, Jumbo, is that we're already between a rock and a ton a' German shells and we're not gannen anywhere fast –

Robbie – apart from our graves.

Will Now imagine we de this, survive, and make it home. What d' y' think happens then?

Jumbo We gan doon the shipyards?

Will Oh no, Jumbo. Nee shipyards for us.

Jumbo I was looking forward t' the shipyard.

Robbie No, you weren't, lad!

Jumbo I was!

Will We become more than that, Jumbo, we become heroes. Think aboot it. The famous singing soldiers. Like the sound of that, divn't ya? Just imagine, our faces on posters across Sunderland, hell, across the country, with the words 'We need you' beneath, or better yet: 'Hero'. Tell us y' divn't want that.

    Beat.

Robbie And all we have t' de is sing?

Will That's all. Y' could think of it like a concert.

    Beat.

Robbie A concert?

Will Aye. A good old fashioned concert. Y' ever done one of those?

Robbie Have I ever . . .? Have I ever . . .? Oh, Will, y' de tickle me sometimes. A concert? Have *I* ever dun a concert?

Will Well, have ya?

Robbie Oh Will, I've dun concerts you wouldn't believe!

Will Aye?

Robbie I've dun concerts the like a' which have never been seen before! I've dun concerts that will gan doon in the Bible they're so good!

Will Aye?

Robbie Oh, I've dun concerts! I've dun concerts!

Jumbo Gan on, Robbie! Gan on, Robbie!

Robbie (*getting tuneful*) I'm off t' de a concert!

He begins an improvised jig and music-hall routine around the idea of putting on a concert. Initially reluctant, Jumbo eventually gets swayed by the joy of it all, as does Will. For a moment we see them as they were, three excitable friends at the back of class, enjoying the madness of each other's company. Robbie finishes in spectacular fashion. He bows with his helmet, the others clap. A gunshot rings out.

Will Doon!

They all hit the deck.

Jumbo What was it?

Will Sniper, I think.

Jumbo Aimed at us?

Will gestures to Robbie, who is still in another world.

Will At him probably.

Robbie Oh, lads! This could be it! Our big break! This could make us stars! Just think of it, lads: the fame! The bright lights! The girls! The suits! The fame! The bright lights! The girls! This could be the big break we've been waiting for! *I've* been waiting for! Singing soldiers! Oh Will, y' clever lad! Always knew I'd de well sticking wi' yee! Never had a doubt, lad! Never a doubt!

Will So you're in?

Robbie All the way.

Will Jumbo?

Jumbo Just like old times?

Will Just like old times.

Jumbo cheers.

Jumbo Smashing! Let's say it.

Will What?

Jumbo The pledge. Now's the time when we say it. We had a really good build-up just then. We should say it now. Ready? Ne killing.

He is alone.

Jumbo Lads! Come on! Ne killing!

Rob *and* **Jumbo** Anly singing.

They look at Will.

Jumbo Will?

Will Jumbo...

Jumbo Please, Will. As a friend. Help us.

Will nods.

All Ne Killing, anly singing, and we all gan home together.

Jumbo cheers again.

Robbie Never thought I'd hear you say that again, Will. Now, if we're ganne de this we're ganne de it properly and that means we need one final thing . . .

Will and Jumbo look at him.

A name.

Will Oh God . . .

FOUR

Robbie and Will on opposite sides of the trench, both in 'thinking' poses. Jumbo sat in between them.

Jumbo The Muddy Choir!

Both look at him.

Robbie *and* **Will** What?

Jumbo The Muddy Choir! That's the name! The Muddy Choir!

Beat.

Robbie Really?

Will What's wrong with it? I like it.

Robbie It's a bit rubbish.

Jumbo It's not!

Robbie Aye, Jumbo, haway, it's propa dull.

Will Look, it took us an hour t' find it so let's just stick with it.

Robbie (*moaning*) Will . . .

Will Good work, Jumbo. Well done.

Jumbo Cheers, Will!

Will turns back to the front.

Robbie Robbie Mitchell and the Thunderstrikes!

Jumbo and Will moan.

What?

Will We already have a name, Rob.

Robbie Robbie Mitchell's Sabre-Toothed Marching Band!

Jumbo That's terrible.

Robbie No, Jumbo, it's amazing. It's *amazing*, Jumbo.

Jumbo I divn't understand the sabre-toothed part, why is there a sabre-tooth in it?

Robbie Because it's ferocious, Jumbo, like us! I can't believe I have t' explain these things t' you!

Jumbo Sabre-tooth's divn't sing, Rob.

Robbie Neither d' muddy choirs, Jumbo!

Will This one does.

Jumbo Aye, this one does!

Robbie Jesus! All right, fine.

Beat.

Muddy Bloody Marys?

Will *and* **Jumbo** No!

Robbie Fine! Muddy Choir! Stupid Muddy Choir!

A whistle. They all scrabble to the trench top and wait, listening intently.

Robbie How many was that?

Will Just one, I think.

Robbie We have t' gan on three?

Will Aye.

Jumbo Is this it?

Will Listen.

They listen.

Robbie I hope it's not cos we haven't properly rehearsed yet . . .

Will Shut up, Rob! I'm trying t' listen.

Again they listen.

Just one.

Robbie False alarm.

They relax back into the trench.

That was a bit tense, wasn't it?

Will notices Jumbo breathing heavily.

Will Jumbo, y' alreet?

Jumbo Aye, just got a bit scared, that's all.

Will Here, have a biscuit. That'll make y' feel better.

Will passes Jumbo a biscuit. He eats it.

Better?

Jumbo nods.

Want anything else?

Jumbo Let's say the pledge.

Will Not now, Jumbo.

Jumbo Please.

Will Mebbes in a bit.

Jumbo Why?

Will If you say it all the time it loses its meaning.

Jumbo You told me I could say it whenever I felt in trouble.

Will That was on the train to basic after we left y' mam and y' wouldn't stop crying.

Jumbo I didn't want to leave . . .

Will Nobody wanted to leave! Why do you two have such a problem understanding that? Y' have t' play the hand y' dealt. Y' cannet live in an imaginary world. Y' have to live in the one y've got and make the best of it! We're in a trench now. Different rules.

Jumbo But you said . . .

Will I kna what I said, Jumbo!

An awkward silence.

Robbie Oh, look, what time it is!

They both look at him.

Band practice time!

Will No. We're stood to.

Robbie We're always bloody stood to. We can sing whilst we're stood to, can't we?

Robbie and Jumbo look at Will. Will sighs his acceptance. They take up positions.

Now let's keep it nice and quiet t' start with. I kna when we get into it and the harmonies kick in we'll start swinging but we have t' resist the urge to fly away with it. We divn't want them kicking off too early, remember. Right, all ready?

They nod.

Here we go . . . One, two, three . . .

Another gunshot.

Will Stand to!

They all scramble for cover.

Robbie For Chris'sake! Won't y' give us a bloody break! We're trying t' run a bloody choir here!

Will Rob, shut up!

Robbie Nah, I'm ganne give them a piece of my mind! I'm sick of this!

He stands up to call over to the other trench.

Oi, lads! Some of us have got important business here! How d' ya expect us t' run a bloody choir when whenever we start rehearsing you start firing! It's not bloody cricket, is it? Why divn't y' just come awer here and have a go like!

He rolls up his sleeves and makes an exaggerated fighting posture towards the enemy.

Bring it on, lads, bring it on!

Will drags Robbie down.

Will What y' deing? Div y' wanna get shot?

Robbie Oh, thanks, Will! I never knew y' cared!

He dusts himself down.

Right, now that battle's won, onwards t' rehearsals! First things first . . .

Robbie pulls out sheet music from his coat.

Song choice!

Jumbo Where did y' get these from?

Robbie taps his nose.

Robbie I have my ways, Jumbo. I have my ways.

FIVE

Robbie, Jumbo and Will stand singing in the trench.

Robbie No, no, no, Jumbo! Y' sound terrible!

Will Rob . . .

Robbie Look, I kna y' struggling with all this but y' really have t' sing in tune. It's the most important part of three-part harmony, Jumbo. In fact it's the only important part!

Will Maybe we should have a little break, eh? We've been at this for hours.

Robbie I divn't understand what's happened to you, y' could de this fine back home!

Jumbo I was in tune, Rob.

Robbie No, y' weren't! I heard it with my own ears, Jumbo! Me own ears! You've got rusty with the lack of practice, but then again y' were hardly a virtuoso before!

Jumbo I can sing as well as any man here!

Robbie No, y' cannet sing as well as any man here cos y' cannet sing as well as us! That's why y' sing bass, Jumbo. Simple, simple, bass. (*He sings.*) Baa, baa, baa. That's you doon there. (*He sings again.*) Baa, baa, baa. Simple. See?

Jumbo I wasn't off!

Robbie Were too!

Jumbo Was not!

Robbie Were too!

Jumbo Was not!

Robbie Were too!

Jumbo Was not!

Robbie Fine! Who else could it be then, Jumbo?

He gesticulates wildly to indicate the lack of people in the trench. Jumbo looks around; he sees Will and points at him.

Will?!

Will It wasn't me, Jumbo.

Jumbo I kna. I'm sorry, Will. I had to pick someone . . .

Robbie *Will?!*

Will Divn't worry aboot it, mate . . .

Robbie I cannet believe this lad sometimes! Y' ganne drive us t' an early grave, Jumbo! If this war doesn't kill us, you certainly will!

Jumbo Fine! It wasn't Will! I divn't kna who it was! All I'm saying is that it wasn't us! I sang the right note, Rob. End. Of.

Robbie I'll give you 'End. Of'.

Will Easy . . .

Robbie Alreet, let's put it t' the test shall we? Ready?

They sing again.

Eee, now y' singing the wrong part, Jumbo! That's Will's part! You're doon here!

He sings bass.

Now you try.

Jumbo tries it but gets it wrong.

No, Jumbo! That's not the bass part! The bass part is doon here.

Robbie sings again.

Try again.

Jumbo does but it goes wrong.

Oh God, Jumbo!

Jumbo I divn't like singing bass, it's boring!

Robbie I kna, man! That's the whole point! Neebody wants t' sing bass! It's just something y' born into and hate for ever: like Newcastle.

Jumbo Why can't you sing bass?

Robbie Because I'm the lead singer, Robbie! The front man. The face. The talent. I have t' de all the fancy trills and fancy moves.

He sings and does a twirl to demonstrate his point.

See? That's what the people want.

Will I'm not sure they do.

Robbie Jumbo, the big lad at the back always sings bass. And today that big man is you!

Jumbo Why can't Will sing bass?

Robbie Cos he's a girl and his voice is too bloody high! Haway, Jumbo, you kna this! Will's a tenor! Remember when he tried t' sing bass at the town hall gig?

Will Rob . . .

Jumbo Oh aye, that was funny!

Robbie does an impression of Robbie trying to sing low. Jumbo laughs.

Y' really can't sing bass, Will.

Will Aye, I think we've established that.

Robbie (*laughing*) Funny gig! Funny bloody gig! Priceless . . .

Jumbo Here, y' remember that club we played in Gateshead? The one where they threw the bottles?

Robbie Remember? I've still got the scars!

They laugh. Robbie sings a bit and pretends to be hit by bottles. They laugh even more.

Still, we made a few shillings out a' that one!

Will Aye, and a few hospital trips!

Robbie That's show business, folks!

Jumbo Oh, and y' remember the time Robbie forgot his hair cream and refused to go on?

Will laughs.

Robbie Divn't talk aboot that! It's a sensitive subject!

Will (*doing an impression of Robbie*) I cannet gan on! I cannet gan on, lads! It isn't straight! It isn't bloody straight!

Will and Jumbo fall about laughing.

Robbie Oh, laugh it up, but the hair's an important part of the package!

Will and Jumbo laugh even harder.

Alreet, alreet, well, how aboot that time when Jumbo got stage fright and would only go on if he had a sandwich first? That was stupid, right? That was stupid!

Jumbo and Will look back at him blankly.

Jumbo No. I was hungry.

Will He was hungry.

Beat.

Jumbo Hey, y' remember when we sang together for the first time?

Will Which one was that?

Robbie Y' divn't remember?

Will Not the first one.

Robbie Oh, Will, it was the best! Doon Pennywell Working Man's Club. Jumbo's mam got us up on stage t' de a turn. Jumbo got stage fright and started crying and then your dad laughed at him and when the bouncer threw him out you had nowhere else to gan so Jumbo's mam got you up onstage with us.

Will (*sarcastic*) Oh, aye, the good old days . . .

Jumbo That wasn't the first time we sang.

  Both look at Jumbo.

That was the first time we were on stage together, but we didn't sing then.

Robbie He's right. We just stood there awkwardly until Jumbo stopped crying and then I did my funny walk act.

  He prepares to do the act, but Will *holds up a hand to stop him.*

Will Wait, I've got it! The first time we sang was the Sunday after when we sat next to each other in church. It was the first time we hung out together and when Jumbo shared his boiled sweets the vicar shouted at us for disrespecting Christ.

Robbie (*laughing*) Oh, aye! (*As vicar.*) 'Jesus never ate sweets and neither shall you!'

  Robbie and Will *laugh.*

Jumbo That wasn't it.

  They look at him.

That was with other people. The first time we sang alone was when we snuck round the fence during break, waited till everyone went in for lessons, and then Rob taught us 'Parting Glass'.

Robbie smiles.

Robbie Y' remember it?

Jumbo It's my favourite.

Jumbo clears his throat. He sings the first line and slowly the other two join.

PARTING GLASS

Of all the money that e'er I spent
　I've spent it in good company
And all the harm that e'er I've done
　Alas it was to none but me
And all I've done for want of wit
　To memory now I cannet recall
So fill to me the parting glass
　Good night and joy be with you all.

Of all the comrades that e'er I had
　They are sorry for my going away
And all the sweethearts that e'er I had
　They would wish me one more day to stay
But since it falls unto my lord
　That I should rise and you should not
I'll gently rise and I'll softly call
　Good night and joy be with you all.

They finish. It has clearly affected them.

Robbie Well, I think we've found our opening number.

Will nods. They realise Jumbo isn't talking.

Will Jumbo? Y' alreet?

Jumbo shakes his head.

What's wrong, lad?

Jumbo I cannet sing it.

Robbie What? Why?

Jumbo I divn't want t' say.

Robbie We have t' sing it! It's the best song!

Will Easy, Rob. Give him some space.

Robbie What is this, Jumbo? You were up for it a minute ago! Haway, lad! Let's bash it oot again! Stop being such a sissy!

Jumbo No!

Robbie Why?

Jumbo It reminds us of home!

They all stop.

I'm gannen along the line.

He exits. They watch him leave.

Robbie Moody.

Will Jesus, Robbie.

Robbie What?

Will Y' divn't have to push him so much?

Robbie It's how you get stuff done, Will. Success divn't come easy.

Will (*sighing*) Only got room for one up there, haven't you?

He taps the side of Robbie's head, then goes back to looking over the front.

Robbie Ahhh, he'll forgive us when we're stars.

Robbie combs his hair and Will shakes his head in disbelief.

SIX

Robbie is awake, busy preparing himself for the day's rehearsals and laying out sheet music. The other two are asleep. Once he is happy, Robbie crows like cockerel. The other two scramble to their feet.

Will Stand to! Stand to!

Will grabs his rifle and hastily takes up position. Jumbo, slower to rise, rubs his eyes as he stumbles around for his own weapon.

Jumbo Are we under attack?

Robbie Even better. It's band practice!

Both turn to him.

Will What?

Robbie holds out sheets for them.

Robbie Here are y' sheets for the day.

Will For God's sake, Robbie, I though we were being attacked!

Robbie Y' need t' calm y'self doon then, Will! Think aboot what's happens t' y' blood pressure when y' get all stressed out like this, eh? It's not good for ya, I'm tellin y', lad! We need t' get y' oot a' this war and quick!

Jumbo Div we really need t' de it this early?

Robbie points aggressively at the two of them.

Robbie Look, lads. If we're gannen to our deaths singing then we're bloody well deeing it properly. I'm not dying on a bad harmony. Nee bloody way. That means we need t' sound perfect and the only way t' sound perfect is what, Jumbo?

Jumbo Practice?

Robbie Exactly! And you for one need plenty of it!

Will Y' could have gone for a more gentle wake-up, Rob.

Robbie Aye, and where's the fun in that?

Will (*sighing*) I've created a monster . . .

Robbie Now, I think we're all agreed we had a great session yesterday and it looks like 'Parting Glass' is the one –

Jumbo raises his hand, but Robbie pushes it back down.

– so I took the liberty of preparing some more complicated harmonies for it. We'll start with that this morning and see how we get on, if y' really good then I'll let y' have a listen to me solo in the afternoon. Oh, y' lucky devils you!

Jumbo Where d'y' get these from?

Robbie taps his nose.

Robbie I have my ways, Jumbo. I have my ways.

Will Oh God.

Robbie Jumbo, it's good t' see y' back and finished wi' y' paddy. We were starting t' think you might never return. Mother here was getting very worried.

Will Aye, Jumbo, tell us next time y' gannen off. Even if y' gannen off in a huff I need t' kna. I cannet protect y' if I divn't kna where y' are, can I?

Jumbo nods.

Robbie Thanks, Captain.

Will opens his mouth to object but Robbie drives on.

Now before we get started we're ganne de a bit of a warm-up. We divn't want t' ruin our voices before the big day, so that means scales, scales, scales. I've prepared some special one's f' the occasion that I think y' might like. Ready? Copy after me. (*To the tune of an ascending scale.*) Gas gas gas gas gas gas gas gas. (*And then descending.*) Gas gas gas gas gas gas gas gas. All together.

All (*ascending scale*) Gas gas gas gas gas gas gas gas. (*Descending.*) Gas gas gas gas gas gas gas gas.

Robbie Beautiful! Now some quick raspberries on a machine gun.

> *Robbie makes the sound of a machine gun: tongue and lips' articulation. The others copy.*

A couple sirens on an alarm.

> *Nasal sirens, ascending and descending. Robbie first and then the boys join in.*

Wonderful! Now, let's pick up our sheets and turn t' page . . .

> *Jumbo steps away, shaking his head and looking at the floor.*

Jumbo I cannet de it.

> *Robbie and Will look at Jumbo.*

I had a dream last night. I was on the pitch in the middle of Roker Park and me mam and the Angel Gabriel were there and they both telt us not t' sing so I'm not ganne sing.

> *Pause.*

Robbie Give him a biscuit.

Jumbo No! I divn't want any biscuits!

Robbie Alreet, this is serious.

A whistle. They all stop, listen and wait. Another whistle.

Will Positions! Stand by!

Will and Robbie prepare themselves. Jumbo doesn't.

Jumbo!

Robbie Jumbo, get ready!

Jumbo No!

Robbie Jumbo!

Will Wait!

Will holds up a hand.

Listen . . .

They listen. There is no third whistle.

Robbie How many was that?

Will Two.

Robbie Y' sure?

Will Aye.

They relax.

Robbie Jumbo, y' didn't join us.

Jumbo I telt you I couldn't. I had a dream aboot the stadium, me mam and Gabriel . . .

Will Well, Jumbo, that means y' breaking the pledge.

Robbie and Jumbo look at Will.

Jumbo What? No, I'm not.

Robbie Aye, I divn't think he is, Will . . .

Will No, he is. If he's not singing that means he's killing and he divn't want t' gan home with us.

Jumbo That's not true . . .

Will Your pledge, Jumbo, your rules.

Jumbo Divn't say that, Will! I'm not breaking it! I'm just not singing.

Will Well, I'll just have t' tell the Sergeant Major we can't go through with the plan and then he'll put us court martial. All three of us will go up in front of a firing squad and it'll be your fault.

Jumbo Divn't tell him, Will! Please!

Will I'll have nee choice, Jumbo. There's nee other way. It's that or y' chop y' leg off and getting invalided off the line.

Jumbo looks at his leg.

Robbie Haway, Jumbo, stop looking at y' leg like that!

Jumbo looks back up at them, distraught.

Jumbo I . . .

Will Who was y' ma's favourite, Jumbo? Out of all three of us?

Beat.

Jumbo You.

Will Why?

Jumbo Because you let us copy y' homework, and y' stopped the lads bullying Rob for his hair, and when they used t' pick fights wi' me to test their strength you'd send 'em packing.

Will Aye. And who'd y' ma tell y' t' trust now, Jumbo?

Beat.

Jumbo You.

SEVEN

Jumbo asleep in the trench. Will cleaning his rifle. Robbie looking out over no-man's-land.

Robbie I cannet see anything. It's too dark.

Will Y' eyes will adjust in time.

Robbie I've been looking for hours and it's all still black.

Will Well it is night-time, so that might have summit t' dee with it.

Robbie What am I looking for?

Will Signs of enemy activity.

Robbie What does that mean?

Will Flashes.

Robbie They're flashing? Waheey, cheeky boys! At least they're having fun, eh!

Will Not flashing. Flashes. Reflections of metal. They might be trying t' sneak up to us.

Concerned, Robbie looks at Will.

Robbie Sneak up on us?

Will continues cleaning.

Will Aye. That's how they dee it. Sneak up t' the wire when it's dark, all nice and quite like, snip it open and then when y' not looking, slip awer the side, doon into the trench and cut y' throat while y' sleeping.

Robbie looks at Will. It's clear he has never considered this before.

Robbie For real?

Will Aye, it's happened before. You should listen t' the briefings, y' might learn a thing or two.

Robbie How d'we stop 'em?

Will points to the front.

Will Keep looking.

Robbie turns back to no-man's-land, this time with a renewed sense of fear. He tries to hold it for a minute but it's too much.

Robbie Will?

Will pretends not to hear.

Will?

Still Will ignores him.

Will!

Will Shhh! Keep y' voice doon will ya? You'll wake Jumbo!

Robbie Y' wanna take awer?

Will Had enough?

Robbie nods. Will smiles.

Not as easy as it looks, is it?

Robbie Will y' bloody swap already?

They swap places. Robbie settles on to the floor, clearly relieved. Will takes up his familiar position.

Will Better?

Robbie Much.

Robbie settles himself, pleased to be back within the relative safety of the trench floor.

So, how d' y' think it's gannen?

Will Not great. Probably be another six months till we break the stalemate. Ypres will be a hard fight too. Every attempt to take her has failed. Apparently there's a plan t' tunnel under their line and plant explosives, the explosion will blow 'em sky high and the Krauts will be defenceless.

Robbie No, Will. I meant the band.

Will Oh, right. Aye, great. I think it's gannen great.

Robbie Today was a bit of a mess though, wasn't it? I mean, Jumbo was all awer the place.

Will Y' got t' de y' rehearsal, didn't you? Be grateful for that.

Robbie I divn't think we can call that a rehearsal, Will. It's hardly much use when two lads are singing and the other one's just mumbling along.

Will Got through it though, didn't we? That's the important thing.

Robbie Aye, but Jumbo's hardly on top form, is he? And y' laid it on a bit thick with him back there. Threatening t' tell the Sergeant Major? That's dark, Will.

Will Just deeing what you couldn't, lad. Getting the job done nee matter the cost.

Robbie Oh aye, you're good at that, Will. I'll give you that.

Will We need t' keep him under control. Y' can see in his eyes he's losing it. He cannet hold a rifle without shaking and spends half his time looking at that bloody picture of his mam. One of us needs to be with him at all times. If he tries t' run we need t' be ready.

Robbie Worried he'll end up in front of a firing squad?

Will looks at Robbie.

That would be bad news, wouldn't it, Will? For him, obviously, but for you too cos you'd probably end up pulling the trigger.

Will (*urgent whisper*) Shut up, Rob! Shut up now!

Robbie Oh, imagine Jumbo's face then! Shaking in his boots, he's hauled up in front of the firing squad and when he musters enough courage to look his executioner in the eye he sees you, looking right doon y' sights at him . . .

Will Rob, we had an agreement! You promised t' keep y' mouth shut!

Robbie Oh, it's alreet, Will. I kna. I remember. I remember what y' said and I remember y' said y'd only de it once. A one-off. Extraordinary circumstances.

Will Aye.

Robbie And you've only done it once, haven't you?

Will Aye.

Robbie So there's nothing t' worry aboot, is there?

Will No. Everything's grand.

Robbie Everything's just grand . . .

Will turns away.

Mind you, imagine if Jumbo found out what you'd done? That'd push him right awer the edge, wouldn't it! You kna, if he found out you'd shot a man . . .

Will Y' ganne tell him, Rob? Is that y' big plan? What d'y' think will happen then, eh? He runs. The band fails. You lose y' only way home and any chance a' success. You want that t' happen?

Robbie is silent.

No? Then think aboot the big picture for once!

Robbie (*sheepishly, knowing he has nothing else left*) You still killed that lad . . .

Will That boy was ganne die nee matter who pulled the trigger! What does it matter if it was me or another lad in that firing squad? Sometimes y' need t' get y' hands dirty t' take care of y' mates. Otherwise we might as well just throw ourselves awer the bloody top and have done with it.

He waits for Robbie's response. There is none, so Will turns back to the front.

Robbie You ever think aboot it?

Will Think aboot what?

Robbie Y' kna.

Robbie gestures at the top of the trench. Will looks up, then back to Robbie.

Will Think aboot what?

Robbie Come on, Will.

Will No, say it. I want you t' say it if y' think it's such a good idea.

They look at each other.

Robbie Helmet off. Cigarette in mouth. Stand up. Bang.

Will scoffs.

Will And I thought Jumbo was the idiot.

Robbie Y' telling me y've never thought aboot it? Ever?

Will doesn't respond.

I thought so.

Will You ever think aboot where you'd end up?

Robbie What, Hell? It cannet be worse than the bombs and the rats and the gas, can it? In fact they've probably got smaller rats.

Will checks his watch.

Will Well, de it if y' like but I'm not giving up.

He steps down from the post.

Robbie Where y' gannen?

Will Duty. Stay here and keep an eye on Jumbo.

Robbie What duty can you have now? It's the middle of the night!

Will Special duty.

Robbie (*sarcastic*) Oh, well, that's cleared that up!

Will Sergeant Major's expecting me.

Robbie Aye, cannet be late for him!

Will It's important.

Robbie It always is whenever you scuttle off.

Will exits. Robbie watches him go.

EIGHT

Jumbo alone. He has clearly been crying. Will enters. He hastily wipes away his tears.

Will Where's Robbie?

Jumbo shrugs.

God, I'm gonna kill that lad when I see him! Y'alreet? Y' not supposed t' be alone.

Jumbo Aye.

Will Good. Best start getting y' things together.

He begins preparing himself. Jumbo does not.

I've just spoken t' the Sergeant Major and he says the attack is imminent. Apparently the Krauts are moving artillery into position by the woods and they've been throwing smoke all morning so chances are we'll go earlier than thought.

Jumbo Will? D' y' get scared when y' sing?

Will Haway, lad, start getting ready, will ya?

Jumbo I do. I get scared inside. You ever feel that? As soon as I start singing, as soon as I hold a note, I feel myself shaking inside, I hear the note wobbling and I want t' cry. I kna it's wrong, I kna I'm soft, but I cannet de it without shaking. It's like everything comes up, everything that was doon comes up. I can't de it like I used te.

Will Divn't worry aboot that now, Jumbo, we've got more important things t' be deeing.

Jumbo Who d' y' shoot at?

Will stops in his tracks, believing Jumbo has found him out.

Will What?

Jumbo When we have t' fire at the German lads. Who d'y shoot at?

Will Oh, I . . .

Jumbo I shoot right awer their heads. I aim just past them, just t' the side, or sometimes dead in the wrong direction. Is that what you de?

Will nods.

Will Aye.

Jumbo I thought so. Y' ever think aboot them?

Will The Germans?

Jumbo Aye.

Will I think aboot what they're planning, where they might be, when they might be looking at us. Watching us.

Jumbo I think aboot what they're having for suppa. I wonder if they've got suppa at all. I wonder what they think when they hear us sing. I wonder why they bomb us because of it. I wouldn't bomb us if I heard singing. I would just listen t' it. Even if it was Germans.

Will Well, you're different, Jumbo.

Jumbo I'm sure some of them are the same.

Will Maybe.

Jumbo I divn't want t' be shot at any more, Will.

Will I kna, mate.

Jumbo You seem really strong oot here. I'm really proud of you. So is Rob. I kna he doesn't show it like but we're really grateful for you looking oot for us like this. I divn't kna what I'd de without the two of you.

Will pulls a can from his jacket.

Will Hungry?

Jumbo Where d' ya get that?

Will Privilege a' rank.

He begins opening the tin.

What d'y' think it is: biscuits or ham?

Jumbo We should wait for Rob.

Will We should wait for Rob, but we're not ganne. I think ham.

54

Jumbo I hope not. The ham here tastes funny.

Will That's because there's a fundamental difference between the ham we have here and the ham they have back in Sunderland.

Jumbo Really?

Will For sure. You see the Sunderland ham is made of ham. Which comes from?

Jumbo thinks.

Jumbo A pig.

Will Correct. And our trench ham comes from?

Jumbo A trench pig?

Will Close.

Beat.

Rats.

Jumbo Rats?

Will That's right, you heard me correctly: rats. Our ham is made of rats.

Jumbo inspects the can.

Jumbo Is that why they divn't have wrapping?

Will Exactly.

Jumbo What's German ham made of?

Will Naughty rats.

Jumbo nods sagely.

Jumbo Makes sense.

Will That's trench life f' ya, Jumbo. If y' not eating rats –

Robbie returns.

Robbie – y' not eating. He trying t' convince you the ham is rats?

Jumbo It is, Rob, we just figured it out.

Robbie And what other lies has he been telling you?

They pause, the change in Robbie's tone apparent to all.

Will Where've y' been? Y' kna y' not supposed t' leave Jumbo on his own. We had an agreement, y' said you'd watch him while I was gan.

Robbie Oh no! Wouldn't want t' break an agreement, would I? Wouldn't want t' gan back on a promise. A pledge. Oh no! Wouldn't want t' de that now, would I?

Jumbo Robbie, what y' talking aboot?

Robbie I've just come from a lovely little meeting wi' our Sergeant Major. See, I was walking along the line trying t' prepare meself for the big day –

Will – when y' shoulda been watching Jumbo –

Robbie – and what do I see? None other than our very own Will popping oot a' his dugout. Intrigued by all the lovely things you'd said aboot him I thought I'd pop in and see what was happening. And oh, was he chatty, Will! Oh, so chatty! I had nee idea! Nee wonder y' wanna spend all y' time wi' him rather than us!

Will Rob . . .

Robbie Y' see, we got t' talking, and he couldn't wait to talk aboot his favourite subject, Will: you. Oh, he loves you, Will. Said you were the best most loyal soldier he ever had. Never let him doon, he says. Aye, I says. That's our Will. Never lets anyone doon, always dependable. Then he says you was just in there and I'd just missed you.

Will Divn't –

Robbie So, I asked him where y' ganne on y' special duties and he telt me, Will. He telt me all aboot the special duties you've been deing. He says, 'Oh, divn't y' kna? Will's our most trusted lad. Always turns up for special duties. Time after time. Done more than anyone else. Probably a record-breaker,' he says.

Jumbo What's he talking aboot, Will?

Robbie You want t' tell him or should I?

Jumbo Tell us what?

Robbie Tell him what special duties are. Tell him how y' got y' stripe.

Jumbo He got it because he's responsible. He's the leader.

Robbie Oh, lied t' him as well, did ya?

Jumbo He's not a liar, Robbie.

Robbie I'm sorry t' bring doon y' hero, Jumbo, but there's a lot y' divn't kna aboot our Lance Corporal here.

Jumbo That's not true. Will doesn't keep anything from us. D'ya, Will?

Will is silent.

Robbie Oh, poor Jumbo. Y've nee idea.

Jumbo Will?

Robbie Not ganne say anything?

Jumbo Will?

Robbie Will?

Will I shot a man.

Pause.

Robbie One of us.

Pause.

Will I served on a firing squad. I shot a man, one of our own. A deserter. He refused t' fight and tried t' run. Sergeant Major asked for a detail t' tie him up and lay rounds into him. I did it.

Pause.

Jumbo He made y' de it?

Robbie No, Jumbo, he volunteered. Our Will volunteered.

Will I didn't want t' de it, but the Sergeant Major offered us a promotion. Bumped us up to Lance Corporal, got us extra rations and got us off the line: got us this.

Robbie What do you mean 'got us this'?

Beat.

Will This was his position. This was his post.

Horrified, Jumbo jumps to his feet.

Robbie You're a monster, Will . . .

Jumbo This was his post?

Will Jumbo . . .

Jumbo Oh God . . .

Robbie And he wasn't the only one was he? Sergeant Major says you've been at it again and again and again. In fact, I bet that's where y' snuck off t' last night, wasn't it?

Will is silent.

Robbie I knew it! Y' gonna need longer sleeves t' fit all the stripes on y' arm!

Will That's not what it is, Rob. He offered us a promotion t' serve in the regimental headquarters. Back away from the line.

Jumbo You were ganne abandon us?

Will I was ganne gan there and then bring you with us. Get us all properly transferred oot away from the line. For ever.

Robbie And what about the singing? Is that all part of this too? Get us to agree to sing and he'll make you a bloody general will he?

Will Robbie, if I'd told ya, y'never would have agreed.

Robbie Too bloody right!

Will Y' see? This is exactly why I couldn't tell you!

Jumbo That lad y' shot. He was innocent just like us? He just wanted t' gan back t'his mam like us?

Will He was gannen aboot it the wrong way, Jumbo.

Jumbo Would y' have shot me, Will? Would you have shot me if I'd run?

Will Course not, lad! I did it t' protect ya!

Jumbo How is he different, Will? How is he different!

Will I . . .

Jumbo Would y' de it again, Will? If y' could dee it all again. Would ya?

    Pause.

Will Aye. If it meant getting both a' you oot a here, I'd de it again. I'd de it again in a flash, again and again and again.

Robbie Murderer.

Will Take that back.

Robbie No.

Will picks up his rifle.

Will Take that back.

Robbie Oh, finally! Come on, lad! How long have y' been waiting t' de that?

Jumbo Put it doon, Will! We're friends!

Will He's not my friend!

Robbie What y' ganne de, big man? Shoot us just like that other poor lad? Where d'y' de him, Will? Was it here? Was it right here where I'm standing? Is this bringing back memories, lad?

Will I'll de it, Robbie. So help me God, I'll de it.

Robbie Oh y' bloody love this, divn't ya? Captain Army Man With a Big Gun! Lay it on then, lad! Lay it on, Will! I'm ready!

Will I'll shoot you, Robbie!

Robbie I want you te!

Will I will, I'll de it!

Robbie I'm saying yes! De it! I want y' te! I want you t' shoot me!

Jumbo Will! Please!

Robbie De it because I'm sick of this place, I'm sick a' this bloody choir and I'm sick a' you!

Jumbo Rob!

Robbie Murderer!

Will Rob . . .

Robbie Liar!

Will reloads the rifle.

Haway, lad, you've always wanted ta! Here's y' chance. Get y' last obstacle t' promotion oot the way!

Will raises the rifle at Robbie's face.

Will Take it back!

Jumbo snatches the rifle from Will's hands and turns it on him.

Robbie Jumbo!

Shaking, Jumbo holds the rifle to Will's face.

Jumbo?

Still shaking, Jumbo looks at the rifle in his hands.

Jumbo . . .

Jumbo drops the rifle.

Jumbo, it's alreet, mate . . .

Jumbo exits. Robbie and Will look at each other.

NINE

Robbie is asleep in the corner of the trench. Will is watching him. Jumbo enters. Will sits up.

Will Alreet.

Jumbo nods.

Where've y' been?

Jumbo Walking.

Beat.

Will Listen, Jumbo, I wanted t' apologise aboot before . . .

Jumbo D'ya think we're ganne make it home, Will?

Will's lack of an answer says enough. Jumbo has made up his mind. He takes a moment to steel himself. He takes out the picture of his mum and kisses it. Placing it back in his pocket he turns to Will. There is a calmness, a stillness in him now that was not there before.

Can I have a cigarette please, Will?

Will Y' divn't smoke.

Beat.

Jumbo Can I have a cigarette?

Will looks at Jumbo.

Please.

Pause.

Will No.

Jumbo I'd de it for you.

Will No, Jumbo . . . not like this . . .

Jumbo Are we friends?

Will Divn't ask us me that, Jumbo . . .

Jumbo Friends help each other, Will.

He extends his hand.

Help me. Please. One cigarette.

Jumbo doesn't move, his hand held out steady. Slowly Will takes the cigarette packet from his jacket and holds it out for Jumbo. Jumbo reaches for it, but Will grabs his hand and pulls him to the floor. Jumbo screams out and attempts to fight back.

Will Divn't ever ask that of us! Robbie! Robbie!

Robbie wakes to see the chaos on the floor.

Robbie What the . . .

Will Help me!

Robbie jumps on and they all wrestle.

Robbie What's he deing?

Will Being an idiot!

Jumbo Let me go!

They force Jumbo up against the trench wall and pin him there. All breathing heavily, they are exhausted.

I want t' gan home! I divn't want t' be here any more! I want t' gan home! Let me gan home! I hate it here! I hate this war! I hate this place and I hate myself! I'd rather be dead than be here! I wish I was dead!

Will Y' not gannen anywhere, Jumbo! Y' staying right here wi' y' mates! Isn't he Rob?

Will turns to Robbie.

Isn't he, Rob?

Robbie nods.

Say it, Robbie! Say it so he knows!

As Robbie opens his mouth we hear a pop and a hiss. All stop. Collectively they realise what has happened.

Robbie *and* **Will** Gas! Gas! Gas!

Robbie and Will race to unpack their gas masks. As they tear through handles and pouches they fail to notice Jumbo is making no effort to get his own.

Jumbo Thank you for everything, boys, you've been the best friends a lad could ever ask for.

The boys looks up at Jumbo.

Robbie *and* **Will** Jumbo!

Jumbo I'm coming home, Mam!

They jump on him but it is already too late. Jumbo begins to cough and splutter. He takes large gasps of air and through the cries of his friends we see him convulsing. His body heaves one final time, the last stirrings of life leaving him, then rests. There is a moment of silence. Robbie cries out.

Robbie Cowards! Y' bloody cowards!

Robbie hits the walls of the trench. Will remains silent and still, looking at his dead friend as Robbie slides to the ground. Will cries in the corner.

TEN

Will and Robbie sit. Holding their rifles against their chests, they wait. Silence. Jumbo's body has been removed. Will takes a paper and pencil from his jacket.

Robbie What's that?

Will We have t' write summit t' his family. To his mum.

Robbie Now?

Will The attack is aboot t' start. We might not get another chance. In fact we should probably de our own after.

Will prepares to write.

Robbie What y' ganne tell her?

Will I divn't kna.

Robbie Y' ganne tell her he's dead?

Will The War Office will de that. We need t' say summit comforting, summit personal.

Robbie Aboot how he died?

Will Aboot how he lived.

Robbie Are we ganne lie?

Will Why would we lie?

Robbie Because he was unhappy. Y' wanna make him sound happy?

Will I need t' tell her summit.

He puts pencil to paper and looks at Robbie.

What do I say?

Robbie sits forward, clears his throat and searches for the words.

Robbie Dear Jumbo's mum . . .

Robbie trails off. Will waits for him to continue. Robbie looks at Will.

This is really happening, isn't it?

A whistle from off. They both look up.

Will First whistle.

Will checks his watch.

They're starting early.

Will turns his attention back to the page.

Dear Jumbo's mum. By now you will have heard that Jumbo . . . James . . . passed away on . . . what's the date?

Robbie I divn't kna.

Will Y' divn't kna?

Robbie No. D'you?

Will turns back to the paper.

Will . . . passed away during November 1917, in a trench in Belgium. Do I tell her how?

Robbie shakes his head.

In a trench in Belgium. He was with his mates . . . and thought of you.

Beat.

Condolences, William and Robert.

Will looks at the paper one final time and then folds it up.

Robbie What d'we de now?

Will Follow orders.

Second whistle.

Second whistle.

Will takes up his position and begins humming a scale.

Robbie So this is it?

Will continues preparing himself.

Will?

Will Aye.

Robbie Jumbo's gone.

Will looks at Robbie, who is on the verge of tears.

Jumbo's gone.

Will I kna.

Robbie Divn't leave me.

Third whistle. Silence. Will looks to the top and then back to Robbie. Slowly he lays his rifle to the floor.

What y' deing?

Will removes his helmet.

Will Div'ya think I'm a bad man, Rob?

Robbie Will, the third whistle's gan!

Will I've just lost one best mate and I'm not aboot t' lose another.

Robbie Will, that's three whistles! That's the signal!

Will I've done things I'm not proud of, Robbie. Terrible things. I've killed unarmed boys and armed boys, I've killed boys that just wanted t' gan home and boys that wanted t' kill us. I've killed boys like you and me. And I kna God will see t' me cos of that, but y' have to kna, everything I did, I did for us. T' get us home. T' get all three of us home. I always knew that whatever happened, it would be the three of us together. Whether it was just three lads shooting at a chalk net drawn on a school wall in Sunderland or three lads trying t' hold a tune in a trench in France, it was always ganne be the three of us. And that's what I telt meself. But y' cannet be like that oot here, Rob. Y' cannet be any kind a' way oot here. It's just madness, that's all it is, just bloody madness. I'm sorry you had to be here and I'm sorry I had to be here and I'm sorry Jumbo had t' be here too. We were sent and that's that. Doesn't make it fair and doesn't make it right but y' kna what, Jumbo knew it all along. There are only three things that really matter in this world. Nee killing.

Will looks at Robbie.

Nee killing . . .

Beat.

Robbie Anly singing.

Beat.

Both And we all gan home together.

Robbie removes his helmet.

Nee killing.

Robbie places his rifle on the floor.

Anly singing.

Bombing starts.

And we all gan home together!

Bombs and whistles can be heard.

Nee killing!

Anly singing!

And we all gan home together!

Loud bomb. They both cower.

Robbie Ah dinnet think y' a bad man, Will.

Will Thanks, lad.

Another bomb.

Robbie Our lads are getting bombed, Will.

Will I kna.

Robbie We should have sung.

Will A choice between lads dying on one hand and lads dying on another is ne choice, Rob.

Robbie What about y' promotion? Getting off the line?

Will I'm done. This is their war not mine.

Robbie Y' kna we'll get court-martialled for this? Firing squad.

Will If we survive the bombs.

Robbie Aye, if we survive the bombs.

Will And either way we'll de it together. There's only one way I'm leaving this trench and that's with you, Robbie. We're not gannen anywhere. We're staying here, together, right? Mates?

Will extends his hand. Robbie takes it.

Robbie Mates.

Will clears his throat.

Will Now, some flash git once telt me man's got a right t' sing and nee war can take that away from him.

Robbie laughs.

One more for old times' sake?

Robbie They won't hear us. The bombings already started.

Will I kna. This one's just for us.

Will smiles. So does Robbie.

Robbie Jumbo's favourite?

Will Y' sure? It's a girl's tune.

Robbie laughs. More bombs and whistles. A cacophony of sound. They duck, it's clear the end is imminent.

Take it away.

Robbie For Jumbo.

Will For Jumbo.

Robbie One, two, three, four . . .

PARTING GLASS

Of all the money that e'er I spent
   I've spent it in good company
And all the harm that e'er I've done
   Alas it was to none but me
And all I've done for want of wit
   To memory now I cannet recall
So fill to me the parting glass
   Good night and joy be with you all.

Of all the comrades that e'er I had
   They are sorry for my going away
And all the sweethearts that e'er I had
   They would wish me one more day to stay
But since it falls unto my lord
   That I should rise and you should not
I'll gently rise and I'll softly call
   Good night and joy be with you all.